PARALLEL EXTRACTS

FROM

FORTY-FIVE MANUSCRIPTS

OF

Piers Plowman.

PARALLEL EXTRACTS

FROM

FORTY-FIVE MANUSCRIPTS

OF

Piers Plowman,

WITH NOTES UPON THEIR RELATION TO THE SOCIETY'S
THREE-TEXT EDITION OF THIS POEM.

BY THE
REV. WALTER W. SKEAT, M.A.,

THE EARLY ENGLISH TEXT SOCIETY

Great Clarendon Street, Oxford OX2 6DP
United Kingdom

Oxford University Press is a department of the University of Oxford.
It furthers the University's objective of excellence in research, scholarship,
and education by publishing worldwide. Oxford is a registered trade mark of
Oxford University Press in the UK and in certain other countries

© The Early English Text Society 1866

The moral rights of the authors have been asserted

Database right Oxford University Press (maker)

First Edition published in 1866

All rights reserved. No part of this publication may be reproduced,
stored in a retrieval system, or transmitted, in any form or by any means,
without the prior permission in writing of Oxford University Press,
or as expressly permitted by law, or under terms agreed with the appropriate
reprographics rights organization. Enquiries concerning reproduction
outside the scope of the above should be sent to the Rights Department,
Oxford University Press, at the address above

You must not circulate this book in any other form
and you must impose this same condition on any acquirer

Published in the United States of America by Oxford University Press
198 Madison Avenue, New York, NY 10016, United States of America

British Library Cataloguing in Publication Data
Data available

Library of Congress Cataloging in Publication Data
Data available

Original Series, 17

ISBN 978-0-85-991807-7

INTRODUCTORY NOTICE.

The former edition of " Parallel Extracts from twenty-nine MSS. of Piers Plowman " was published by the E. E. T. S. in 1866, in the form of a thin tract containing 16 pages. Instead of reprinting this tract in its original form, I take the present opportunity of making it more complete, though at the same time I omit certain remarks which are no longer of importance.

The former edition may be thus briefly described. It began by requesting all who were interested in the Poem to assist me in the endeavour to obtain a *complete* list of the MSS., and to ascertain, as far as practicable, the general character of each. At Mr. Furnivall's suggestion, the passage of the Poem corresponding to lines 1508— 1529 in Wright's edition, 1856, vol. i. p. 47, was selected as a test-passage, and an appeal was made for copies of this passage from every known MS. In answer to this appeal, extracts from 29 MSS. were obtained. The Rev. H. O. Coxe kindly supplied extracts "from [most of] the Oxford Bodleian MSS., and Mr. W. Aldis Wright those from the Cambridge University Library and Trinity College; whilst the editor contributed those from Corpus and Caius Colleges, and from the Oxford colleges, and Mr. Furnivall was responsible for the British Museum extracts, the dates of the MSS. of which were kindly fixed by Mr. E. A. Bond, of the MS. department, whose valued help is here gratefully acknowledged. The Dublin extract was kindly furnished by Dr. Lottner."

I then proceeded to shew that the texts of the poem are really *three*, rather than *two*, as generally stated. I also said that the numbering of the Passus differed in various MSS., so that we find Passus VI beginning in three distinct ways, viz. either with the words "Bote ther wer fewe men so wys," or with "This were a wikked way," or "Thus ich a-waked, wot god;" see pp. 32, 33, 34 below. These varying types of the Poem I called, respectively, the *Vernon* type (as being contained in the Vernon MS.), the *Crowley* type (as agreeing with the text printed by Crowley in 1550), and the *Whitaker* type (as agreeing with the text printed by Whitaker in 1813). I have since briefly denoted them by the names A-text, B-text, and C-text, the first of these being the earliest, and the last the latest version, in point of time. I then pointed out numerous variations between the B-text and C-text, which it is now needless to recapitulate, and drew particular attention to the following passages, viz. (1) A. iii. 67—77; B. iii. 76—86; C. iv. 77—85; (2) B. xiii. 264—271, which helps to fix the date of the B-text; (3) C. vi. 1—108, which is peculiar to the C-text; (4) B. iii. 188—204, which alludes to Edward's wars in Normandy; and (5) C. xxi. 283—296, which contains an allusion to *guns*, and should be compared with Milton, Paradise Lost, vi. 470. A short table was added showing the different arrangement of the Passus in the B-text and C-text. Finally, I gave the "parallel extracts" from 29 MSS., the MSS. thus illustrated being those which I have since denoted by the following numbers, viz. I. II. III. IV. V. IX. X. XIII. XV. XVIII. XIX. XXI. XXII. XXIII. XXIV. XXV. XXVI. XXVII. XXIX. XXX. XXXIII. XXXIV. XXXV. XXXVI. XXXVII. XXXIX. XL. XLI. XLII.[1]

I have now to thank many kind helpers for the great success of our appeal. No less than *sixteen* MSS. were afterwards pointed out to me, or were observed by myself in various catalogues. The most important of these were the following. In the Bodleian Library, MSS. Douce 323, Ashmole 1468, Rawlinson Poet. 137 and 38, Bodley 851, and Douce 104. Mr. Yates Thompson sent me an account of an excellent MS. in his own possession, which proved of great service. Lord Ashburnham kindly shewed me his two MSS., both of which are now in the British Museum. The Earl of Ilchester's MS. turned out to be of the highest interest, and the loan of it was most acceptable and helpful. Other MSS. were the MS. in Lincoln's Inn, the MS. in Trinity College, Dublin, marked D. 4. 12, MSS. 8231 and 9056 in the possession of Sir Thomas Phillipps; and, at a later period, the Historical MS. Commission brought to light the MSS. belonging to the Duke of Westminster and Sir H. Ingilby, which are more particularly described at pp. 25 and 28 below. By the kindness of the librarians and owners, every facility has been afforded to me for inspecting all the MSS. of any value. Indeed, I have carefully examined every MS. personally, with only two exceptions, viz. MSS. VIII. and XLI. The former of these was sufficiently described to me by Mr. Furnivall, and the latter by Professor Dowden. To all who have given me such hearty assistance I am deeply grateful.

With these few remarks, I beg leave to submit my completed set of "Parallel Extracts" from *all* the known MSS. of the Poem.

[1] These were, however, arranged in *a different order*, as follows: I. XV. XXIII. XXIV. XIII. XXII. II. XXV. IX. IV. III. XVIII. XIX. XXVI. V. X. XXVII. XXI. XXXIII. XXIX. XXXVI. XL. XXXIX. XXX. XLI. XXXVII. XXXIV. XXXV. XLII.

BRIEF ACCOUNT OF
THE MANUSCRIPTS OF PIERS PLOWMAN;
WITH PARALLEL EXTRACTS.

THE seventeenth publication of the E. E. T. S. was my edition of "Parallel Extracts from twenty-nine manuscripts of Piers Plowman," published with the view of obtaining further information about the MSS. and their contents.[1] This led to further discoveries, and has enabled me to describe many more than those there noticed, and at the same time to do so more fully. I now take the opportunity of printing a more complete set of these "parallel extracts," so as to give some notion of the general appearance of the spelling, &c. of the various MSS.

Owing to the finding of new MSS., the numbers used in the former edition of parallel extracts are no longer available. Even the "roman" numerals given to the MSS. in the three Prefaces do not strictly express the correct order, when we come to compare the MSS. in the exactest manner possible. I arrange them below in such a way as to show which MSS. are most closely related to each other, but retain, for convenience, the "roman" numerals which have already been assigned to them. Many of the MSS. are also indicated, in the footnotes, by capital letters; and I now give tables, showing what the "roman" numerals and the capital letters represent. The MS. marked no. XLV (below) has not been mentioned before.

LIST OF MSS. DESCRIBED IN THE PREFACES.

Nos. I—XII and nos. XLIV, XLV belong to the A-text. Of these, nos. I—X are described in vol. i. pp. xv to xxiv; no. XI is described in vol. i. p. 142*; no. XII in vol. ii. p. vi, footnote; no. XLIV in vol. iii. p. 1, and at p. 25 below; and no. XLV at p. 28.

Nos. XIII—XXVIII belong to the B-text. Of these, nos. XIII—XXVII are described in vol. ii. pp. vi to xxx; and no. XXVIII is described in vol. iii. p. xix, footnote.

Nos. XXIX—XLIII belong to the C-Text. They are described in vol. iii. pp. xix to l.

---

[1] The present publication takes the place of a second edition of this no. 17, which, in its original form, is now out of print.

But this is only a first approximation to the real values of the MSS., and is only assumed for convenience. As a fact, some MSS. are of a *mixed* character. There is a set in which the former part belongs to the A-text, and the latter to the C-text; and another set in which the former part belongs to the C-text, and the latter part to the B-text. We thus get a more exact classification, as follows:

A-text. Nos. I. II. IV. VI. VII. VIII. IX. XI. XII. XLV. (*Ten.*)
B-text. Nos. XIII. XIV. XV. XV* (i. e. the lost MS. printed by Crowley) XVI. XVII. XVIII. XIX. XX. XXI. XXII. XXVI. XXVII. XXVIII. (*Fourteen.*)
C-text. Nos. XXIX. XXX. XXXI. XXXII. XXXIII. XXXIV. XXXV. XXXVI. XXXVII. XXXVIII. XXXIX. XL. XLI. XLII. XLIII. (*Fifteen.*)
Mixed text; A and C. Nos. III. V. X. XLIV. (*Four.*)
Mixed text; C and B. Nos. XXIII. XXIV. XXV. (*Three.*)

NAMES OF THE MSS., AS NUMBERED.

I. Vernon MS., Bodleian Library. (A-text.)
II. Harleian MS., no. 875; B. M. (A-text.)
III. MS. Trin. Coll. Cam. R. 3. 14. (*Mixed;* A and C.)
IV. Univ. College, Oxford. (A-text.)
V. Harleian MS., no. 6041; B. M. (*Mixed;* A and C.)
VI. MS. Douce 323; Bodleian Library. (A-text.)
VII. MS. Ashmole 1468, Bodl. Library. (A-text.)
VIII. Lincoln's Inn, London. (A-text.)
IX. Harleian MS., no. 3954; B. M. (A-text.)
X. MS. Digby 145, Bodl. Library. (*Mixed;* A and C.)
XI. MS. Rawlinson, Poet. 137, Bodl. Library. (A-text.)
XII. MS. Trin. Coll. Dublin, D. 4. 12. (A-text.)
XIII. MS. Laud Misc. 581, Bodl. Library. (B-text.)
XIV. MS. Rawlinson, Poet. 38, Bodl. Library; 4 leaves of which are bound up in MS. Lansdowne 398, in the British Museum. (B-text.)
XV. MS. Trin. Coll. Cam. B. 15. 17. (B-text; printed by Wright.)
XV*. MS. printed by Crowley. (*Lost.*)
XVI. Mr. Yates Thompson's MS. (B-text.)
XVII. Ashburnham MS. no. 129. (B-text.)
XVIII. Oriel College, Oxford. (B-Text.)
XIX. MS. Camb. Univ. Library, Ll. 4. 14. (B-text.)
XX. Ashburnham MS. no. 130. (B-text.)
XXI. MS. Camb. Univ. Library, Gg. 4. 31. (B-text.)
XXII. MS. Camb. Univ. Library, Dd. 1. 17. (B-text.)
XXIII. MS. Bodley 814, Oxford. (*Mixed;* C and B.)

MANUSCRIPTS OF PIERS PLOWMAN. 5

XXIV. MS. Additional 10574 ; B. M. (*Mixed;* C and B.)
XXV. MS. Cotton, Calig. A. xi ; B. M. (*Mixed;* C and B.)
XXVI. Corpus Christi College, Oxford. (B-text.)
XXVII. Caius College, Cambridge. (B-text.)
XXVIII. MS. Phillipps 8252 ; at Cheltenham. (B-text.)
XXIX. MS. Phillipps 8231. (C-text.)
XXX. MS. Laud 656 ; Bodl. Library. (C-text.)
XXXI. MS. Bodley 851. (C-text.)
XXXII. The Earl of Ilchester's MS. (C-text.)
XXXIII. MS. Cotton, Vesp. B. xvi ; B. M. (C-text.)
XXXIV. MS. Camb. Univ. Library, Ff. 5. 35. (C-text.)
XXXV. MS. Corpus Christi Coll. Cambridge, no. 293. (C-text.)
XXXVI. MS. Camb. Univ. Library, Dd. 3. 13. (C-text.)
XXXVII. MS. Digby 171, Bodl. Library. (C-text.)
XXXVIII. MS. Douce 104, Bodl. Library. (C-text.)
XXXIX. MS. Digby 102, Bodl. Library. (C-text.)
XL. Harleian MS., no. 2376 ; B. M. (C-text.)
XLI. MS. Trin. Coll. Dublin, D. 4. 1. (C-text.)
XLII. Royal MS., 18. B. xvii ; B. M. (C-text.)
XLIII. MS. Phillipps 9056. (C-text.)
XLIV.[1] The Duke of Westminster's MS. (*Mixed;* A and C.)
XLV.[2] MS. belonging to Sir Henry Ingilby, of Ripley Castle, Yorkshire. (A-text.)

LETTERS DENOTING VARIOUS MSS.

Some of the above MSS. are denoted in the footnotes and elsewhere by letters. In the A-text, the letters employed are V, H, T, U and *U*,[3] H2, D, and A. They denote the first seven MSS. (I to VII) in the above list, and are chosen as representing the words Vernon, Harley, Trinity, University, Harley, Douce, and Ashmole.

In the B-text, the letters employed are L, R, W, Y, O, C2, C, and B. They denote MSS. XIII—XVI, XVIII, XIX, XXII, and XXIII in the above list, and are chosen as representing the words Laud, Rawlinson, Wright,[4] Yates-Thompson, Oriel, Cambridge (no. 2), Cambridge, and Bodley.

In the C-text, the letters employed are P, E, Z, I and *I*,[5] M, F, S, G, and K. (Also B and T, which, as being *mixed* texts, have been already mentioned.) These letters denote MSS. XXIX—XXXVII in the above list. Most of them can be remembered by connecting

[1] Some account of this MS. is given below ; see p. 25.
[2] Some account of this MS. is given below ; see p. 28.
[3] The italic letter *U* is used to denote the variations in a certain passage (Pass. ii. 1—23) which occurs *twice* in the MS.
[4] Because Mr. Thomas Wright printed this Trinity MS. *in extenso.*
[5] The italic letter *I* is used to denote the variations in a certain passage (C. x. 75—281) which occurs *twice* in the MS.

them with the word they are meant to symbolise; but a few are arbitrarily chosen. Thus P, I, M, K represent, respectively, Phillipps, Ilchester, Museum,[1] Kenelm-Digby. F represents MS. Ff. 5. 35 (Camb. Univ. Library). S is the *last* letter of Corpus. Only E (= Laud 656), Z (= Bodley 851), and G (= Camb. Univ. Dd. 3. 13) have no symbolic meaning. I had intended to use N to denote MS. Harl. 2376, but it was not worth collating.

The above letters, when arranged in alphabetical order, are as follows.

A. MS. Ashmole; no. VII. (A-text.)
B. Bodley 814; no. XXIII. (*Mixed;* C and B.)
C. Cambridge; no. XXII. (B-text.)
C2. Cambridge (later MS.); no. XIX. (B-text.)
D. Douce 323; no. VI. (A-text.)
E. Laud 656; no. XXX. (C-text.)
F. Ff. 5. 35, in Camb. Univ. Library; no. XXXIV. (C-text.)
G. Dd. 3. 13, in the same; no. XXXVI. (C-text.)
H. Harl. 875; no. II. (A-text.)
H2. Harl. 6041; no. V. (*Mixed;* A and C.)
I. Ilchester; no. XXXII. (C-text.)
K. Kenelm-Digby 171; no. XXXVII. (C-text.)
L. Laud Misc. 581; no. XIII. (B-text.) *Adopted as the text.*
M. Museum MS.; Cott. Vesp. B. xvi; no. XXXIII. (C-text.)
N. HarleiaN MS. 2376; no. XL. (C-text.)
O. Oriel MS.; no. XVIII. (B-text.)
P. Phillipps MS. 8231; no. XXIX. (C-text). *Adopted as the text.*
R. { Rawlinson MS. Poet. 38. } No. XIV. (B-text.)
   { Lansdowne 398. }
S. CorpuS MS. Camb.; no. XXXV. (C-text.)
T. Trinity MS. R. 3. 14; no. III. (*Mixed;* A and C.)
U. University Coll., Oxford; no. IV. (A-text.)
V. Vernon MS., Oxford; no. I. (A-text.) *Adopted as the text.*
W. MS. printed by Wright; no. XV. (B-text.)
Y. Mr. Yates Thompson's MS.; no. XVI. (B-text.)
Z. MS. Bodley 851; no. XXXI. (C-text.)

I may add that "Cr.", in the notes to the B-text, stands for Crowley; and that "Whit.", in the notes to the C-text, stands for Whitaker. Whitaker printed his edition from MS. P.

SPECIMENS OF PARALLEL EXTRACTS FROM THE VARIOUS MSS.

⁎ The passage selected for illustration is A. iii. 67—77; B. iii. 76—86; C. iv. 77—85.

[1] The only good example of the C-text in the (British) Museum.

MANUSCRIPTS OF PIERS PLOWMAN.

Text A; sub-class *a*. Printed as the Text, as far as xi. 180; denoted by **V**.
  I. MS. Vernon, in the Bodleian Library; described in Pref. A. p. xv. The best text, but imperfect at the end. It occasionally omits necessary lines. The dialect in which the poem was first written has been *modified by a Southern scribe*.

"¶ Meires and Maistres · and ȝe þat beoþ mene
Bitwene þe kyng and þe Comuns · to kepe þe lawes   68
As to punisschen on pillories · or on pynnyng stoles
Brewesters · Bakers · Bochers and Cookes
For þeose be Men vppon Molde · þat most harm worchen
To þe pore people · þat al schal a-buggen   72
¶ Þei punisschen þe peple · priueliche and ofte
And recheþ þorw Regatorie (*sic*) · & Rentes hem buggeþ
With þat þe pore peple · schulde puten in heore wombe
¶ For toke þei on trewely · þei timbrede not so hye   76
Ne bouȝte none Borgages · beo ȝe certeyne"

Text A; sub-class *a*. Collated; denoted in the footnotes by **H**.
  II. MS. Harl. 875; described in Pref. A. p. xvii. Imperfect, having lost vi. 52—vii. 2, and all after viii. 144. Contains some lines not found in other copies; agrees more closely than any other copy with the text of the preceding MS.

"ȝe meyres & maysters · þat beoþ ordeyned meenes
by-twene þe kynge & þe comyns · þe lawe for to kepe   68
to ponysche on pylorye · & on pynynge stoolis
Brewesteres & bakers · bochers and Cokes
For þese ben men on molde · þat moost harme worchen
to þe pore peple · þat al most abyggen   72
For þei pylen þe pore pepul · priuely & ofte
& waxen ryche regratoures · & rentes hem byggen
wiþ þat þe pore peple · schuld putt in her wombes
ffor if þei token with trouthe · þei tymburyd not so hye 76
ne shulde bye noo burgagis · be ȝe certeyn."

[The foot-note to Text A, p. 31, ll. 71, 72, is wrong.]

Text A; sub-class *b*. The only copy which contains the whole of Passus xii, and from which that Passus is therefore printed.
  XI. MS. Rawl. Poet. 137; described at p. 142* of A-text. Many of its readings resemble those of MS. IV; and it retains the passage x. 205—xi. 47, which is wanting in that MS.

"Meyrys and maysteres · ȝe þat beþ mene
by-twyche þe king & þe common · to kepe þe lawes   68
As punschin on pylorijs · and on pynnyng stolys
breweres bakeres · bocheres and kokes
For þes are men on molde · þat most harme werkyn
to þis pore puple · þat parcel mele beggen   72
for þey poysone þe puple · pryuyly wel ofte

8   MANUSCRIPTS OF PIERS PLOWMAN.

> and rechyn þorw regratyng · and rentes hem buggen
> Of þat þe pore puple · schulde pote in her wombes
> for ne tok he on trewely · he tymbred not so hye   76
> ne bouȝte none bargayns · be þou wel certeyne "

Text A; sub-class *b*. Not collated.

XII. MS. Dublin D. 4. 12; described in a footnote in Pref. B. p. vi, as it was not at first discovered to be of the A-text. Imperfect, ending at vii. 45. Some of the text is transposed, nearly as in MSS. XI and IV. Closely resembles MSS. XI and IV, particularly the former; but is much corrupted in places, whilst *the dialect has been turned into Northumbrian.*

> " Mayres & mercers þat er þe menes
> Bitwix þe kyng & þe comons to kepe þe lawes   68
> For punyschyng on pilorys or pynyng stolys
> Baksters & bowchers brewsters & kukez
> For þees er men of þis molde þat most wrong wirkis
> Tharfore pure peple þair part sare abysse [1]   72
> For þai poson þe pèple preualy full ofte
> And riche þorow regratery rentis þaim byes
> With þat at þe peple suld put in þair wambe
> For toke þai trewly þai temberd noght so hye   76
> Ne boght þai no Burgage be þou full certañ "

Text A; sub-class *b*. Collated; and denoted in the footnotes by U. A fragment of a different A-text (Pass. ii. 1—23) also occurs in this MS., and is denoted in the footnotes by *U.*

IV. MS. no. 45 in Univ. Coll. Oxford; described in Pref. A. p. xx. Some of the text is transposed, just as in MS. XI. It is also remarkable as containing a few lines of the beginning of Pass. xii, the whole of which occurs in MS. XI only.

> " Meires & macerys · þei þat ben mene
> bytwene þe kyng & his comowns · to kepe þe lawes   68
> As to punysche on pylorie · and pynynge stoles
> Breworis and bakeres · bocheris and cokes
> For þese arn men in þis world · þat most harm wurchen
> To þe pore peple · þat parcel mele biggen   72
> For þei poysene þe peple · priueyly wol ofte
> And richen þurw regratrie · & rentes hem biggen
> Of þat þe pore peple · schuld putten in here wombes
> For ne toke þei so wrongwisly · þei tymbrid not so hie
> Ne bouȝte none bargaynes · be þou wol certayn "   76

Text A; sub-class *b* (?). Not collated, except (recently) throughout Passus xii. 1—83. See p. 29.

[1] I. e. "Therefore poor people sorely a-buy (pay for) their part." *Abysse* = *abyis*, the Northern form of *a-buy*, i. e. buy back, redeem, pay for. But this reading is quite corrupt.

XLV. MS. in the possession of Sir Henry Ingilby, of Ripley Castle, Yorkshire. This MS. is remarkable as containing a large portion of Passus xii, the *whole* of which is found in MS. Rawl. Poet. 137 only. For a fuller description, see p. 28 below.

"Meyres & macers · ӡe þat bene mene
Be-twyxen þe kyng & þe comen · to kepyn þe lawes   68
As to puneschyn on pyloryes · & on pynyng stoles
Bruers & bakers · bochers & kokes
For þis arn men of þis molde · þat moste harm wyrchyn
To þe powre peple · þat parcelmel byggen   72
For þei poysyn þe peple · pryuyly wel ofte
And richyn þer (*sic*) regratry · & rentes hem bygge
Of þat þe pou*er* peple · schulde putty*n* in her wombe
For tokyn he on trewly · he tymbrede nouth so hye   76
Ne bowhtyn hem no burges · be ӡe certeyn"

Mixed text: partly Text A; sub-class *c*. Used to form the Text in xi. 181—303. Collated, and denoted in the footnotes by **T**. Contains also a portion of the C-text; viz. xii. 297 to the end.

III. MS. Trin. Coll. Cam. R. 3. 14; described in Pref. A. p. xviii. Apparently the oldest MS. of this (the largest) sub-class.

"Meiris & maistris · hij þat ben mene
Betwyn þe king & þe comunes · to kepe þ*e* lawis   68
As to puniffchen on pillories · & on pynning stolis
Breweris & bakeris · bocheris & cokes
For þife arn men of þife molde · þat moft harm werchiþ
To þe pore peple · þat parcel mel biggen   72
For þei poisone þe peple · preuyly wel ofte
And risen vp þoruӡ regratrie · & rentis hem biggen
Of þat þe pore peple · shulde putte in here wombe
For tok he on trewely · he tymbride not so heiӡe   76
Ne bouӡte none burgages · be ӡe wel certayn"

Mixed Text: partly Text A; sub-class *c*. Partly collated, and denoted in the footnotes by **H2**. Contains also a portion of C-text, viz. xii. 297 to the end.

V. MS. Harl. 6041; described in Pref. A. p. xx. It is remarkably like MS. III (above), but certainly of later date.

"Meyres and maystres / hij þat ben menene dwelly*n*
Betwene þe kyng and þe comyns / to kepe þe lawes   68
As to ponyschen on pileries / and on pynny*ng* stolis
Breweris and bakers / bochers and cokes
For þese arn men of þis molde / þat most harme worchiþ
To þe pore peple þat / parcel mel biggeth   72
For þei poysone þe peple / priuily wel ofte
And risen vp þoruӡ regratrie / and rentis he*m* biggen
Of þat þe pore peple / schuld put in here wombe
For took he but trewly / he tymberid nat so hye   76
Ne bouӡte non bargages / be ӡe wel certayn."

10   MANUSCRIPTS OF PIERS PLOWMAN.

Mixed Text: partly A-text (slightly amplified); sub-class *c* (?). Contains also a part of Text C : viz. Pass. xiii—end.
XLIV. MS. in the possession of the Duke of Westminster. See Pref. C. p. l. Not collated.[1]

"ȝe Mairs and maistres · þat beþ menes
Be-tweyn þe kyng and þe comunes · to kepe þe lawes   68
As to ponyshe on pelorie · or pynnyg (*sic*) stole
Bakers and brewers · bochers and cokes
This ben men on þis mold · þat most harm worchen
To þe pore peple · þat parcelmele biggen   72
For þei appose [*altered to* appresse] þe peple · ful priuyly oft
And beþ riche by regratrie · & rentes hem byggen
Of þat þe pore peple shold · putte in here wombe
For[2] toke þei on treuly · thei tymbred not so hye   76
Ne bought no burgage · be ȝe wel seure"

Text A; sub-class *c*. Partly collated, and denoted in the footnotes by **D**.
VI. MS. Douce 323, in the Bodleian Library; described in Pref. A. p. xxi. An inferior copy, and full of blunders. Contains Prologue and Pass. i—xi.

I had intended to observe, in describing the MS., that some of the matter in it is transposed. Thus, in Pass. iii, the order is thus : lines 1—79, 143—167, 80—127 (128—142 *omitted*), 143—end.

"Meyres & Maystres · þey þat ben mene
Be-twen þe kyng & þe comunes · to kepe þe lawes   68
As to punysshen on pyloryes · & on pynyng stoles
Brewers & bakers · Bochers & Cokes
For þese ben þe men on þis molde · þat most harm werchen
To þe pore peple · þat parcelmel Beggyn   72
For þey poysoun þe peple · preuely wel ofte
And Richen thoruȝt Regratrie · & rentes hem beggyn
Of þat pore peple · shuld put in here wombe
For tooke þey vntrewlyche · tymbred þey nouȝt so heye   76
Ne bouȝte none burgages · be þou wel certeyn"

Text A ; sub-class *c*. Not collated.
VII. MS. Ashmole 1468, in the Bodleian Library; described in Pref. A. p. xxi. Quoted a few times, when it is denoted by **A**. Imperfect at the beginning; begins at i. 142, and ends with Pass. xi. In some readings it agrees with MS. IX.

"Meyris & maceris ! þat ben þece menis
Be-twyn þe kyng & comouneris ! to kepe þese lawis   68
To ponyschin on pelory ! & on pynyng stolis
Breusteris & baxteris ! bocheris & kokis

---

[1] See further remarks upon this MS. below, p. 25.
[2] Here a later hand has (needlessly) inserted *ne*.

MANUSCRIPTS OF PIERS PLOWMAN. 11

<pre>
Thece arn þe men on þis molde ⸵ most harm werchis
To þe pore puple ⸵ þat parcel-mele bigge   72
For þei prechyn þe puple ⸵ preuyly fol ofte
And rechyn with regatris regratrie (sic) ⸵ & rentis hem byggyn
Of þat þe pore puple ⸵ schuld puttyn in here wombe
Toke þai on treweliche ⸵ þai tymberid not so hye   76
Ne boute no burgace ⸵ þis is certayn"
</pre>

Text A; sub-class *c*. Imperfect; not collated.
VIII. MS. No. 150 in Lincoln's Inn; described in Pref. A. p. xxii. Contains Prologue and Pass. i—viii only. The readings frequently agree with those of MS. III, but many corruptions have been introduced by the scribe's excessive love of alliteration. Perhaps some of it may have been written out from memory, and half-lines supplied from the scribe's own head; as only thus can we account for such a version of A. v. 161—164 as the following :—

<pre>
      "Hykke þe hakeneyman · þat coude wel heue þe coppe,
      Clarice of kockeslane · þat klatre can faste,
      Dawe þer was & dolfyn · & a doseyn othir."
</pre>

The following extract was kindly made for me by Mr. Furnivall.

<pre>
      "Meires & macers ȝe þat beon mad mene
      By-twene þeo kyng & þe comunes to kepe the lawes   68
      As to punyschen on pillories & on pynyng stoles
      Breowesters & baxsters bochers and cokes
      For þeose arn men on þis molde þat most harm worchen
      To þeo pore people þat parcymel buggen   72
      For þey poisen þe people pryueliche wel ofte
      And richen þorgh regraterye & rentes þey buggen
      Of þat þe pore people schulde putte in heore wombe
      For toke þey on treowely þey tymbred not so hyȝhe 76
      No boghten no borgaces¹ beo ȝe wel certayne"
</pre>

A-text, amplified; sub-class *d*. Not collated.
IX. MS. Harl. 3954, in the British Museum; described in Pref. A. p. xxiii. Contains the "council of the rats," belonging to the Prologue of the B-text, and other amplifications. But it ends with Pass. xi. Several passages appear to have been corrupted.

<pre>
      "Meyres & macers · þat meene ben be-twen
      þe kyng & þe comoun · to kepe þe lawe   68
      To pounche on þe pyllary · & on pynynge stolys
      Brusterys & baxterys · bucherys & kokys
      For þese² arn men on erthe · þat most harm werkyn
      To þe pouer puple · þat parcel meel byȝe   72
      For þei poysyn̄ ye puple · priuyly & oftyn
      þei rychyn thorw regratryȝe · & rentys hem byen
      with þat þe pore puple · Xuld put in her wombys
      For toke þei nouth vntreuly · þei xuld nout byggye so heyȝe"
</pre>

¹ *Apparently written* borgates.   ² The "þ" is written like "y."

Mixed Text: partly A-text, amplified; sub-class *d*. Not collated.
X. MS. Digby 145, in the Bodleian Library, described in Pref.
A. p. xxiv. This is an amplification of the A-text, as it contains the
"council of the rats," belonging to the Prologue of the B-text. In
this respect it resembles the preceding. It also contains a portion of
Text C, viz. from xii. 297 to the end, in which respect it resembles
MSS. III and V. It is a poor copy.

<pre>
" Mayers & masters · & thay that bene meane
  Betwene the kyng & the commen · to kepe the lawes   68
  As to ponische on pylory · & on pynyng stoles
  Brewars & bakars · bochars & cokis
  For thay arn men on this molde · that most harme worchen
  To the pore people · that parcelmele beggyn   72
  For thay poyson the people · privylich well ofte
  And Rychen through regraterye · & Rentis hem byen
  Of that the pore people · schuld putt in her wombe
  For toke thay not vntrewly · thay tymberid not so hye   76
  Ne bowghte no burgages · be ye well certeyne "
</pre>

Text B; sub-class *a*. MS. adopted as the basis of the text, and
denoted in the footnotes by **L**.
XIII. MS. Laud Misc. 581 (Oxford); described in Pref. B. p. vi.
The best copy of the B-text, carefully corrected. I still adhere to
my opinion that it may indeed be the author's autograph copy.

<pre>
" ¶ Meires and maceres · that menes ben bitwene   76
  Þe kynge and þe comune · to kepe the lawes
  To punyschen on pillories · and pynynge stoles
  Brewesteres and bakesteres · bocheres and cokes
  For þise aren men on þis molde · þat moste harme worcheth 80
  To the pore peple · þat parcel mele buggen
  ¶ For they poysoun þe peple · prineliche and oft
  Thei rychen þorw regraterye · and rentes hem buggen
  With þat þe pore people · shulde put in here wombe   84
  For toke þei on trewly · þei tymbred nouȝt so heiȝe
  Ne bouȝte non burgages · be ȝe ful certeyne "
</pre>

Text B; sub-class *a* (?). Not collated.
XVII. MS. Ashburnham CXXIX; described in Pref. B. p. xv.
This MS. agrees closely (as far as I have observed it) with the B-text
as printed from MS. XIII. It retains the passage (B. xvi. 56—91)
which MS. XXII and others omit. It has plurals in -*us* occasionally,
and sometimes the verbal-endings -*un* and -*ud* for -*en* and -*ed*.

<pre>
" Meires and macers · þat menes be bitwene   76
  Þe kyng and þe comune · to kepen þe lawes
  To punisshen on pilories · and pynynge stoles
  Brewsters and baksteres · bochers and cokus
  For þise arn men on þis molde · þat most harm worcheth 80
  To þe pore peple · þat parcelmele buggen
</pre>

MANUSCRIPTS OF PIERS PLOWMAN.   13

> For þei poysoun þe peple · priuelicher and ofte
> Þei richen þorw regraterie · and rentes hem biggen
> With þat þe pore peple · shulde putte in hire wombes   84
> For took þei on truly · þei tymbred nouȝt so heiȝe
> Ne bouȝte non burgages · be ye ful certein "

Text B; sub-class *a*; but with additional (genuine) passages, which nearly agree with Text C. Collated throughout, and denoted by **R**.

XIV. MS. Rawl. Poet. 38, in the Bodleian Library; described in Pref. B. p. xi. Four leaves of this MS. are in MS. Lansdowne 398, in the British Museum.

> " Meyres and maceeres ! þat menes ben by-twene.   76
> Þe kyng and þe comoune ! to kepe þe lawes.
> To ponysch vppon pilaries ! and pynynge stoles.
> Brewsteres and bakesteres ! bocheres and kokes.
> For þese aren men vppon þis molde ! þat moste harme werchen. 80
> To þe pouere poeple ! þat parcelmel buggen.
> And al so poysene þe poeple ! priuelich and ofte.
> Þei richen thorȝ regratrie ! and rentes hem buggeth.
> with that þe pouer poeple ! schulde putte in here wombe.   84
> For toke þei on trewely ! þei tymbrede nouȝt so heyȝe.
> Ne bouȝte none burgage ! be ye ful certeyne "

Text B; sub-class *b*. Partly collated, and denoted by **Y**.

XVI.. MS. in the possession of H. Yates Thompson, Esq., of Liverpool; described in Pref. B. p. xiv. A fair text, the spelling of which resembles the printed text, but it has a few various readings, in which it resembles those of the same sub-class.

> " Maires and maceres · that menes ben bitwene   76
> The kyng & the comune · to kepe the lawes
> To punysshen on pilories · and pynyng stoles
> Brewesters and Baxsters · bochers and Cookes
> For thise aren men on this molde · þat most harme worcheth   80
> To the pore peple · that parcelmele buggen
> For they poysen the peple · priuelicher and ofte
> They richen thorugh regraterie · and rentes hem buggen
> With that þe pouere peple · sholde put in hir wombe   84
> For took they on trewely · they tymbred nouȝt so heigh
> Ne boughte non burgages · be ye ful certeyn "

Text B; sub-class *b*. Not collated.

XXI. MS. Camb. Univ. Lib. Gg. 4. 31; described in Pref. B. p. xxiii. A late and sometimes faulty copy from a fair text, which has many readings in common with the preceding.

> " meyres & maces · that meynes be betwene   76
> the kyng & the commvnes · to kepe the lawes
> to punnyſſhen on pylloryes · & pynyng ſtoles

MANUSCRIPTS OF PIERS PLOWMAN.

> brewſters & baksters · bochers and kokes
> for thes are men on thys mold · þat moſt hvrte worchen   80
> to the pore people : that percellmeyle beggen
> for they poyſen the poeple · pryuyleche & oft
> they ryſen thrvgh regratrye · & rentes them byggen
> with that þᵉ poere poeple · ſhvld pvtt In theyre wombes   84
> For tooke they not vntrvely · they tymbred not ſo hye
> ne boght no bvrgagys · by þᵉ certeyne."

Text B; sub-class *b*; imperfect. Collated throughout; see footnotes marked **C**.
XXII. MS. Camb. Univ.̇ Lib. Dd. 1. 17; described in Pref. B. p. xxiii. Remarkable for its omission of the passage in B. xvi. 56—91; for some other omissions, for additions of a few lines of doubtful authority, and for the frequent occurrence in it of Northern forms. See e. g. *worches* in l. 80 below.

> " Maires and maceres · that menes ben bitwene   76
> The kyng and þe comune · to kepe the lawes
> To puniſſhen on pilories · and pynyng ſtoles
> Breweſters and baxters · bowchers and cookes
> For thyſe aren men of this molde · þat moſt harm worches   80
> To the pore pepyle · that percelmele buggen
> For thay- poiſon the pepyle · priuelicĥe and oft
> þey richen thurgh regraterie · and rentes hem buggen
> With þat þe porȩ pepyle · shulde put in hir wombe   84
> For tooke thay on trewely · thay tymbred nouȝt ſo heiȝ
> Ne bouȝte non burgages · be ye ful certeyne."

Mixed Text: part of Text B, sub-class *b*, imperfect; together with part of Text C. See footnotes marked **B** both in B-text and C-text, and some of the Critical Notes, B. pp. 391—395.
XXIII. MS. Bodley 814; described in Pref. B. p. xxv; cf. Critical Note on B. ii. 121, p. 391. Remarkable for its omission of the passage in B. xvi. 56—91; for the mixture of C-text (Passus i, Pass. ii and part of Pass. iii) with B-text (part of Pass. ii and Pass. iii—xx); and for numerous corrupt readings.

> " Maires and maceris · þat menes ben bitwene   76
> þe kyng and þe comune · to kepe þe lawis
> To punische on pilories · and pynyng stolis
> Brewsteris and baksteris · bocheris and cokis
> For þise arn men of þis molde · þat most harm worchiþ   80
> To þe pore peple · þat parcelle mele biggen
> For þei poisone þe peple · priuelyche and ofte
> þei richen þurgh regratrie · and rentis hem bieggen
> Wiþ þat þe pore peple · shulde putte in her wombe   84
> For toke þei on trewely · þei tymbrid not so hiȝe
> Ne boughten none burgagis · bi þe ful certeyne."

Mixed Text: part of Text B, sub-class *b*, imperfect; together with part of Text C. Not actually collated, yet practically represented by the footnotes marked **B** both in B-text and C-text.

XXIV. MS. Additional 10574; described in Pref. B. p. xxvi. This is little else than a mere duplicate of the preceding, and written by the same scribe. The note in Mr. Wright's edition, Introd. p. xxxvii (note 24), as to the identity of this MS. with that used by Dr. Whitaker, is erroneous; see Pref. C. Observe how closely this extract agrees with the preceding, especially in the odd spelling *bieggen* in l. 83, and in the false reading *bi þe* in l. 86.

" Maires and maceris · þat menes ben bitwene   76
The kyng and þe comune · to kepe þe lawes
To punche on pilories · and pynyng stolis
Brewsters and baksteris · bocheris and cokis
For þise arn men of þis molde · þat most harm worchiþ   80
To þe pore peple · þat parcelle mele bieggen
For þei poisone þe peple · priueliche and ofte
þei richen þurgh regratrie · and rentis hem bieggen
Wiþ þat þe pore peple · shulde putte in hire wombe   84
For toke þei on trewely · þei tymbrid not so hiȝe
Ne bouȝten none burgagis · bi þe fulle certeyne."

Mixed Text: part of Text B, sub-class *b*, imperfect; together with part of Text C. Not actually collated, yet practically represented by the footnotes marked **B** both in B-text and C-text.

XXV. MS. Cotton, Caligula A. xi (B. M.); described in Pref. B. p. xxvii. Apparently a copy of one of the two preceding, with both of which it very closely agrees. In the readings *brewsteris* (l. 79) and *her* (l. 84) it follows MS. XXIII, not MS. XXIV.

" Meires and maceris · that menys ben bytwen   76
the kyng and the commune · to kepe the lawes
to punsche on pilories · and pynyng stolis
brewsteris & bakesteris · bocheris and cokes
for these arn men of this molde · that most harm worcheth   80
to the pore peple · that parcelle mele byggen
for thei poysen the peple · priuylich and ofte
thei richen thorgh regraterie · and rentis hym byggen
with that the pore peple · shulde putte in her wombe   84
for tok thei on trewly · thei tymbred nat so hyȝe
ne boughtte none burgages · by the ful certeyne."

Text B; sub-class *c*. Collated throughout, and denoted in the footnotes by **O**.

XVIII. MS. Oriel LXXIX; described in Pref. B. p. xvi. A neat and good copy, of which four leaves have been unfortunately lost, so that the passages in xvii. 96—340, and xix. 276—355 are wanting.

> " Meires & maystres · þat menes been bitwene 76
> þe kyng & þe comunes · to kepe wel þe lawes
> To punyschen on pyleries · & pynynge stoolis
> Breusters & bakesters · bochers & cokis
> For þeise arn men on þis molde · þat moost harm worchen 80
> To þe pore peple · þat parcelmele biggen
> For þei punyschen þe peple · princylich & ofte
> Þei richen þoruʒ regraterie · & rentis hem biggen
> Wiþ þat þe pore peple · schulde putte in her wombe 84
> For toke þei on truli · þei tymbreden not so hye
> Ne bouʒte noon burgages · be ʒe ful certeyn."

Text B; sub-class *c*. Collated wherever the Oriel MS. fails, and denoted by **C2**. See also vol. ii. p. 421.

XIX. MS. Ll. 4. 14 in the Cambridge University Library. Apparently copied from the Oriel MS. when perfect, thus preserving the passages which are wanting in that MS. Comparison of the two copies at once shows many similarities in the spelling.

> " Meyrs and mayftres · menes be bitwyne 76
> The kynge & þᵉ Comunes · to kepe well þᵉ lawes
> To punnyffhen on pyleries · & pynynge ftolis
> broufters & bakers · bocheris and cokis
> For þefe arn men on þis molde · þat mofte harm worchen 80
> To þe pore peple · þat parcellmele biggen
> For þei punnyfchen þᵉ peple · preuylich & ofte
> þei richen þoruʒ regraterie · & rentes hem biggin
> Wíth þat þᵉ pore peple · fhuld put in here wombe 84
> For toke þei on truly · þei tymbred not fo hie
> Ne bouʒte non burgages · be ʒe Full Certeyne."

Text B; sub-class *d*. Most of the important readings are given in the Critical Notes; B. pp. 387—420.

XV.* MS. first printed by Robert Crowley A.D. 1550; *now lost*. See Pref. B. p. xxxi; and p. xiv, footnote 2. The extract is here given as it stands in Crowley's *first* edition.

From 'The Vision of Pierce Plowman, now fyrste imprynted by Roberte Crowley, 1505 [1550].'

> " Maires and Maceris that meanes be betwene 76
> The Kynge and the comon to kepe the lawes
> To punnyshen on pyleries and pynning stoles
> Brusterrs and bakesters, bochers and cokes
> For these ar men on this mold yᵗ most harme worketh 80
> To the pore people that percel mele byghe
> For they poyson the people priuilie and ofte
> They richen thrughe Regratrie & rentis hem bighen
> With yᵗ the pore people should put in here wombes 84
> For toke they all trulie they tymbred not so high
> Ne bought no burgages be they full certen."

MANUSCRIPTS OF PIERS PLOWMAN. 17

The following variations occur in the *second* impression, also dated 1550. 76. *Mayres* and *masters*. 77. *common*. 78. *punnyshe, pylaries, pynnynge*. 79. *Brusters, bouchers*. 81. *percell meale*. 82. *poysen, priuely, oft*. 83. *through regratry, rentes*. 84. *her*. 85. *truely, timbred, hygh*. 86. *be ye*.
The *third* impression, also dated 1550, has all these variations, except that it has *punyshe* (with one *n*) in l. 78; moreover, it has *byghen* in l. 83. The edition printed by Owen Rogers in 1561 has all the variations of the above *third* impression, and these following additional ones. 81. *poore*. 84. *shoulde*. 85. *truly*.

Text B; sub-class *d*. A mere transcript (not quite an exact one) of Rogers's edition of 1561, and therefore a more corrupt copy of the foregoing.
XXVII. MS. No. 201 in Caius College, Cambridge; described in Pref. B. p. xxx. Of no value.

"Mayres and maifters that meanes be betwene 76
The king & the common to kepe the lawes
To punysche on pyluries and pynnyng stoles
Brufters and bakefters bouchers and cokes
For thefe ar men on this mould yat most harme worketh 80
To the poore people that percell-meale bigge
For they poyfon the people privily and ofte
They richen through regratry & rentes hem biggen
With that the poore people fhould put in her wombes 84
For tooke they all truly they tymbrid not fo high
Ne bought no burgages be ye full certen."

Text B; sub-class *d*. Collated throughout; see footnotes marked W. XV. MS. Trin. Coll. Camb. B. 15. 17; described in Pref. B. p. xiii. Printed *in extenso* by Mr. Wright.[1] A remarkably good MS.

"Maires and Maceres · þat menes·ben bitwene 76
The kyng and þe comune · to kepe þe lawes
To punysshe on Pillories · and pynynge stooles
Brewesters and Baksters · Bochiers and Cokes
For þise are men on þis molde · þat moost harm wercheþ 80
To þe pouere peple · þat percelmele buggen
For þei enpoisone þe peple · pryueliche and ofte
Thei richen þoruȝ regratrie · and rentes hem biggen
Wiþ þat þe pouere peple · sholde putte in hire wombe 84
For toke þei on trewely · þei tymbred nouȝt so heiȝe
Ne bouȝte none burgages · be ye ful certeyne."

---

[1] The few *errata* in Mr. Wright's edition are enumerated in Pref. B. pp. xxxvii, xxxviii.

Text B; sub-class uncertain, but either *a, b, c,* or *d.* Not collated.
  XX. MS. Ashburnham CXXX; described in Preface B. p. xxi.
A faulty copy, with attempted "corrections," which seem to be
taken from Crowley's printed edition. It contains also a *fragment*
of Piers the Plowman, viz. B. ii. 208—iii. 72, which is quite distinct
(and different) from the complete copy.

> "Meyres and mercers[1] · that menes ben bytwene   76
> The kyng and the comune · to kepe the lawes
> To punysche on pyloryes · and pynynge stoles
> Brewesters and baksters · bochers & cokes
> For þese arne men of this molde · that moste harme wurcheth 80
> To the poore peple · that parcelmel beggen
> [· . . . .
>   . . . . . . *no gap in the MS.*]
> Wyth that the poore peple · schulde putten in here wombe   84
> For tooke they on treuly · they tymbred nougth so hye
> Ne bouhten no burgages · be ȝe fuH certayn."

Text B; sub-class *e.* Not collated.
  XXVI. MS. Corpus Christi Coll. (Oxford) CCI; described in
Pref. B. p. xxvii. Contains several additional lines, which are often
spurious. The manner of division of the poem into Passus is wholly
different from that of every other MS.

> "Meyȝres wit*h* here Macerys · þat meenys been be-twene 76
> þe kyng & þe Comʷronys · to kepen wel þe lawys
> & punysschyn vpon pylory · & on pynynge stolys
> Boþe websteres & bakesterys · & bocheres & Cookys
> For þo are men vpon moolde · þat mest harm wirche   80
> To þe poore peple · þat percel-meel byggyn
> & poysene þe peple · pryvyly & softe
> þey richen þorou regratrye · & rentys hem byggyn
> wit*h* þat þe·pore peple · sholde pytte in here wombe   84
> For tooke þey on trewly · þey tymbred not so hyȝe
> Ne bowhte no bargayn · be þe fulle serteyn."

Text B; sub-class *f.* With alterations. Not collated.
  XXVIII. MS. Phillipps 8252; described in Pref. C. p. xix; as
it was not at first perceived to belong to the B-type. In fact, it is a
mixed text, being chiefly of the B-type, with a few additions from the
C-text, made in quite a different way to those which appear in MS.
Rawl. 38. This is well shown by the description of "Wrath"
printed by Dr. Whitaker; see my remarks. It is much corrupted,
and of little value.

> "Mayres & macers · that menes are bytwene   76
> Þe kyng & þe comunes · to kepe þe lawes
> Shold ponysshe on pylories · and pynnyng stoles

---

[1] "mercers" is written over an erasure.

MANUSCRIPTS OF PIERS PLOWMAN. 19

Brewers and bakers · bochers and kokes
For þes are men in þis world · þat moost harm warkys   80
To þe pore peple · [. . . . .
. . . . *no gap in MS.*] · pryvily and ofte
Þei wexe riche þurgh regratrye · & bye he*m* meny rentes
Wi*th* þat þat þe pore peple · shold put in here wombe   84
Toke þei on trewly · þei tymbryd not so hye
Ne boght so meny bargaynes · be ȝe wele certeyn."

Text C; sub-class *a*. Taken as the basis of C-text, and denoted
  by **P**.
XXIX. MS. Phillipps 8231 (formerly Heber 973); described in
Pref. C. p. xix. Printed (not without many mistakes) by Dr.
Whitaker, and now reprinted. The best MS. of this type.

"ȝut mede myldeliche · þe meyre hure bysouhte,
Bothe shereues[1] and seriauns[2] · and suche as kepeþ lawes
To punyshen on pillories · and on pynyng stoles
As bakers and brewers · bouchers and[3] Cokes   80
For þees men doþ most harme · to þe mene puple
Richen þorw regratrye · and rentes hem byggen
Whit þat þe poure puple · sholde putten in hure wombeu
For toke þey on triweliche · they tymbrid nat so heye   84
Noþer bouhten hem burgages · be ȝe ful certayn."

Text C; sub-class *a*. Collated throughout, and denoted by **E**.
XXX. MS. Laud 656, in the Bodleian Library; described in
Pref. C. p. xxiv. Almost a duplicate of the preceding. The auto-
type fac-simile issued with vol. iii. represents a page of this MS.

"ȝut mede myldelic*h* ! þe mere ȝo bysouȝt
boþ schereues & seriauns ! & suche as kepeþ lawes
To punyschen on pillories ! & on pynynge stoles
As bakers & breweres ! boucheres & cokes   80
For þ*is* me*n* doþ most harme ! to þe mene peple
Richen þroȝ reg*r*aterie ! and rentes hem biggen
Wi*th* þat þe pore peple ! scholde pute*n* i*n* here women (*sic*)
For toke þey on t*r*ewelic*h* ! þei tymbred noȝt so heye   84
Noþer boȝten burgages ! be ȝe ful c*er*tayn."

Mixed text: partly Text C, sub-class *a*. Denoted by **Z**. Not fully
  collated.
XXXI. MS. Bodley 851; described in Pref. C. p. xxx. A
remarkable MS., agreeing very closely (in the latter part) with the
printed text. But the former part, which approaches the B-type, is
corrupt and valueless. The C-text begins with Pass. xi.

[*The selected passage is not extant in this* MS.]

---

[1] "shereves" *in* Whitaker.   [2] "serjiauns" *in* Whitaker.
     [3] " & " *in* Whitaker.

20   MANUSCRIPTS OF PIERS PLOWMAN.

Text C; sub-class *a*. Imperfect. Collated as far as it goes, and
  denoted by **S**.
XXXV. MS. no. 293 in the library of Corpus Christi College,
Cambridge. Described in Pref. C. p. xli. Observe the forms *askuþ*,
kepun, kokus, buggun, burgagus, &c.

  " ȝut men fcholde leue mede · & do þat refoun afkuþ
    Boþe fchereues & feriauntes · & fwiche as kepun lawes
    To punchen on piloryus · & pynnynge ftoles
    As bakeres & breueres · bocheres & kokus   80
    For þefe men doþ moft harm · to þe comune peple
    Ryche þoruȝ regraterye · rentes hem buggun
    Wiþ þat þe pore peple · fcholde putte in here wombe
    For toke þey fo trewly · þey tymbred nat fo hye   84
    Noþer boghte burgagus · be ȝe ful certayn."

Text C; sub-class *a*. Imperfect. Partly collated; denoted by **G**.
XXXVI. MS. Dd. 3. 13 in the Camb. Univ. Library. Often
resembles the Corpus MS. above. Described in Pref. C. p. xlii.

  " ȝet mede myldely · mayrys by souȝhte
    Boþe fchereuys & seriauntys · and suche as kepyþ lawes
    To punefchen upon pyleryes · & pennynge ftoles
    Afe bakers & brewers · bochers & cokys   80
    For þees men don moft harm · to þe mene peple
    Ryche men þourgh regratrye · & rentys hem biggen
    Wyþ þat þe poure peple · fcholde put yn here wombes
    For tok þey on trewly · þey timbred nouȝt so hyȝe   84
    Noþer bowȝten burgagys · beo ȝeo ful certain"

Text C; sub-class *a*. Not collated.
XLI. MS. D. 4. 1 in the Library of Trinity College, Dublin;
described in Pref. C. p. xlviii.

  " And mede myldely · þe me·re scho by-sowte
    Bothe schereues and sergans · and suche as kepeþ lawes
    To·punyschen on pylorys · and on pynnyngstoles
    As bakeres and brewers · bocheres and kokes   80
    For þes men doþ most harm · to þe mene people
    Rechen throw regraterye · and rentes hem buggen
    With þat þe poere people · schold putten in here wombe
    For tok þei on trewly · þey tymbred nat so hye   84
    Nowþer bowten borgages · be ȝe ful certayn."

Text C; sub-class *a*. The latest MS. of this type, but occasionally
  exhibiting a fair text. Not collated.
XLII. MS. Bibl. Reg. 18 B. xvii, in the British Museum.
[Contains also the "Crede."] Described in Pref. C. p. xlviii.

  " Yet mede myldlich · the mayre she be-sought
    bothe shryves and sergans · and such that kepeth lawes

MANUSCRIPTS OF PIERS PLOWMAN.

> to punyshen on pylloryes · & on pynyng stoles
> As bakers and brewers · Bochers and Cokes   80
> ¹for these are men on this mowlde · that moste harm woorketh
> ¹for they pey to the poore people · that percell meale bighe
> ¹for they poyson the people · pryvely and ofte ·
> They enrichen thorugh regratry · and rent*is* hem bigheń
> with that the pore puple · shulde putten in her wombes
> for toke they on trewly · they tymbredeń nought so hye   84
> neyther boughten no burgages · be ye full certeyne."

Mixed Text: but mostly a C-text, sub-class *b*; from C. ii. 1 onwards. Denoted by **I**. A ·passage in it (C. x. 75—281) occurs twice over; readings from the second copy are denoted by *I*.

XXXII. MS. Ilchester; described in Pref. C. p. xxxiii. Imperfect and peculiar, but of considerable value.

> "ȝit meede þe mayr · myldeliche he bisoghte
> Boþe schirrifs and sergeantz · and suche as kepeþ þ' lawes
> To punyschen vpon pylories · and vpon pynyng stoles
> as bakers and brewers · bochers and Cookes   80
> For these men don most harme · to þe mene peple
> Richen thurgh regraterye · and rentes hem beggeþ
> Wiþ þat þe pouere poeple · schulde putten in here wombe
> For tooke þay on trewely · þay tymbred nat so heie   84
> ne boghten none burgages · be ȝe ful certeyn."

Text C; sub-class *b*. Not collated.

XXXIX. MS. Digby 102, in the Bodleian Library; described in Pref. C. p. xlvi. Imperfect at the beginning, and the lines are written continuously (like prose), but divided into lines by red strokes, and into half-lines by red marks like inverted semi-colons. Begins with the words "of notaries" (iii. 156). Exhibits many readings similar to those of the Ilchester MS. above.

> "ȝut mede the mayre ! myldeliche sche by-souhte /
> Bote Shyreues and Seriauntȝ ! and suche as kepeth lawes /
> To puneschen vȝpen pylories ! and vppon pynyng stoles /
> As bakeres & brewers ! bocheres & cokes /   80
> For thyse men don most harm ! to the mene peple /
> Rychen thorw regraterye ! and rentes hem biggeth /
> With that the pore peple ! sholde putte in here wombes /
> For tok they on trewly ! they tymbrede nat so heye /   84
> Ne bouhte none burghgages ! be ȝe ful certeyn /"

Text C; sub-class *b*. Not collated.

XXXVIII. MS. Douce 104; described in Pref. C. p. **xlv**. Abounds with rudely drawn pictures.

> "ȝit mede þe meyre · mildely be-soȝth
> Boþ shereues & sariauntes · & such as kepeþ þe law ·

---

¹ These *three* lines are reduced to *one* in the C-text proper. Cf. B-text.

22 MANUSCRIPTS OF PIERS PLOWMAN.

> To punchen oppon pilories · & oppon pynnyng stoles[1]
> As bakers & brewers · bouchers & kokes 80
> For þos men doþ most harme · to þe mene pepil
> Ryȝth proȝth regratry · rentes ham byggiþ
> With þat þe pore pepil · schuld put in har wombe
> For tok þei euer trewly · þai tymbrid noȝth so hey 84
> Ne boȝth noȝth burgages · be ȝe ful certayn."

Mixed Text: partly Text C, sub-class *b*. Only in the latter part, beginning at C. xii. 297. Collated from p. 213 onwards. Denoted by **T**.

III. MS. Trin. Coll. Cam. R. 3. 14; described in Pref. A. p. xviii, and Pref. C. p. xxxviii. See p. 9 above.

[*Extract already given.*]

Mixed Text: partly Text C, sub-class *b*. Only in the latter part, beginning at C. xii. 297. Not collated for the C-text.

V. MS. Harl. 6041, in the British Museum; described in Pref. A. p. xx; and Pref. C. p. xxxviii. See p. 9 above. Closely resembles the preceding.

[*Extract already given.*]

Mixed Text: partly Text C, sub-class *b* (?). From C. xiii. 1 to the end. Not collated.

XLIV. MS. in the possession of the Duke of Westminster. Closely resembles the two preceding MSS. See p. 10 above.

[*Extract already given.*]

Mixed Text: partly Text C, sub-class *b* (?). Only in the latter part, beginning at C. xii. 297. Not collated.

X. MS. Digby 145, in the Bodleian Library; described in Pref. A. p. xxiv, and Pref. C. p. xxxviii. See p. 12 above.

[*Extract already given.*]

Mixed Text: partly Text C, sub-class *b*. Only near the beginning, as far as C. iii. 128. Denoted by **B**.

XXIII. MS. Bodley 814; described in Pref. B. p. xxv, and Pref. C. p. xxxviii. See p. 14 above.

[*Extract already given.*]

---

[1] Indistinct; apparently "stokes," instead of "stoles;" due to the next line ending with "kokes."

MANUSCRIPTS OF PIERS PLOWMAN. 23

Mixed Text: partly Text C, sub-class *b.* Only near the beginning, as far as C. iii. 128.
XXIV. MS. Additional 10574; described in Pref. B. p. xxvi, and Pref. C. p. xxxix. See p. 15 above.
[*Extract already given.*]

Mixed Text: partly Text C, sub-class *b,* as above.
XXV. MS. Cotton, Caligula A. xi (British Museum); described in Pref. B. p. xxvii, and Pref. C. p. xxxix. See p. 15 above.
[*Extract already given.*]

Text C; (perhaps) sub-class *a.* A disappointing MS. Not collated; or it would have been denoted by **N**.
XL. MS. Harl. 2376, in the British Museum; described in Pref. C. p. xlvii. It is there shown to be a faulty copy.

"ȝit mede myldely · þe mayr hyre by-sought
Boþ scherefys & seriauntes · & hem þat kepeþ lawes
Some punysseheþ op-on pileryes · & on pynyng stoles
As bakers & brewers · bouchers & koukes   80
For þes men doþ most harm · to þe comen peple
Rycheþ þorow regratrye · & rentes hem bygges
W*ith* þat þe powre peple · scholde put in here wombe
For hy touke so vntruly · hy tymbred nouþ so hyeȝe   84
Some bouȝte burgages · be ȝe ful certayne."

Text C; sub-class *c.* Intermediate to sub-classes *a* and *b.* Imperfect. Partly collated; denoted by **K**.
XXXVII. MS. Digby 171, in the Bodleian Library, Oxford. Described in Pref. C. p. xliii.

"ȝut Mede myldely · marie heo by-souȝt
Boþe fchereues and feriauns · and fuche as kepeþ lawes
To punyfchen vpon þe pilories · and on pynyngſtoles
As bakeres and bruweres · bochours and cokes   80
For þefe men doþ moſt harm · to þe mene people
Richen þourȝ regraterie · and rentes hem biggen
wiþ þat þe poure people · fchulde putten in here wombe
For toke þei truwely · þey tymbred not fo heyȝ   84
Nother bouȝten borgages · beo ȝee fulcertayn."

Text C; sub-class *d.* Approaches more nearly to sub-class *a* than to sub-class *b.* Collated throughout, and denoted by **M**.
XXXIII. MS. Cotton, Vespasian B. xvi, in the British Museum. Described in Pref. C. p. xxxix.

"¶ ȝut mede þat maide · þe meir sche bi-souȝte
Boþe schereues and sergauntz · and swiche as lawes kepen

To punissche on pilaries · and in penyng stoles
As bakers and brueres · bocheres and cokes   80
For þese men don most harm · to þe mene peple
Rechen þorw regratrie · and rentes hem biggen
Wiþ þat þe pore peple · schulde putte in heore wombe
¶ For token þei treweli · þei stieden nouȝt so hiȝe   84
And bouȝten hem no burgages · be þe wel sure."

Text C; sub-class *e*. Varies considerably from sub-classes *a* and *b*. Imperfect; collated as far as it goes; denoted by **F**.
XXXIV. MS. Ff. 5. 35 in the Camb. Univ. Library. Missing passages—C. viii. 265 to x. 181, and C. xiv. 94 to xvi. 178. Described in Pref. C. p. xl.

"But ȝit mede myldely þe meyr heo befouȝte
boþe fchereues & feriauntes and fuche as kepeth lawes
to punyfche on pileryes & on pynnyng ftoles
bakers & brewers bocheres & cokes   80
for þefe doth moft harm to þe commune peple
richen þurw regraterye & rentes hem biggeth
with þat þe pore peple fcholde putte in here wombe
for toke þei al trewly þei tymbred nat fo hye   84
noþer bigge burgages be ȝe ful certayn."

Text C; sub-class doubtful. Not collated.
XLIII. MS. Phillipps 9056 (formerly Heber 974). Described in Pref. C. p. xlix.

"ȝet mede þe maide · mildeliche bisouȝt
Boþe shire-reues and sergauntes · and suche as kepeþ þe lawes
To punishen vppan pileries · & pynyng stoles
Ac (*sic*) bakers and brewers · bochers and cokes   80
For þese men don most harme · to þe mene peple
Richen þruȝ regratrie · and rent hem biggeþ
Wiþ þat þe pore peple · schuld putte in her wombe
For But þei wonne so vntrewly · þei build nouȝt so heiȝe 84
Ne her auncestres neiþer · be ȝe ful certein
Bouȝt non Burgages · ne suche gret places."[1]

[1] The last two lines are corruptly spun out of one line in the original.

DESCRIPTIONS OF MSS. XLIV AND XLV.

XLIV. In the Preface to the C-text, p. 1, I explained that this MS. was not accessible at the time of writing the descriptions of the MSS. I have lately applied again to the Duke of Westminster, who has most courteously allowed me the full use of the MS., so that I am now enabled to describe it accurately, as well as to give the extract printed above.

There are three vellum fly-leaves at the beginning and end, but these form no part of the original MS.; on one of them is written "Richard Grosvenor," in a hand of the seventeenth century.

The MS. itself is neatly written on parchment, in a handwriting of (as I suppose) the former half of the fifteenth century. It consists of 9 quires of 8 leaves each, followed by a quire of 6 leaves; thus the whole number of leaves is 78. The size of each page is 11 inches by 7½ inches, and the usual number of lines in a page is 41. The poem ends on the front of leaf 76, and is succeeded by 7 lines in alliterative verse in a later hand, of no value. At the end is the colophon—Explicit tractatus uiri[1] piers plowman nominatus. Leaves 77 and 78 are blank, as well as the back of leaf 76. The text, like that of MS. T, is not all of one type, but has been made up from two others. The former part is of the A-type, which ends on fol. 31*a* with the line (A. xi. 303)—

Wiþ-oute penance at here partyng · in-to þe hie blysse.

The Latin quotation *breuis oratio penetrat celum* is wanting, though there is just room for one more line on the page. On turning over the leaf we find the line (C. xiii. 1)—

Allas I say quod olde (*sic*) · and holynesse boþe.

The former part of the MS. tends to agreement with MSS. T and D, but the text is somewhat disappointing, with numerous variations and corruptions. Yet the copy must have been made (ultimately at least) from an excellent original, and many of the readings are of considerable interest, at any rate to myself. The very peculiarities of the MS. give it a special value. The scribe sometimes omits lines, amongst which I may notice A. i. 5 (and part of 6), A. i. 168, A. iii. 262, 263, A. v. 96, 163, 167, 197, A. vi. 31, A. vii. 96, 125, 227, 228, 282—284, 286, A. viii. 105, 106, A. ix. 12, A. x. 64, 67, 81, 82, 117, 186, 210; besides the lines which are marked in the footnotes as existing "in H only." But he also *inserts* lines, most of which really belong to the B-text. Thus, in place of A. i. 112, he gives us B. i. 113—116; after A. i. 129, he inserts B. i. 139 (and Latin) and 140; after A. ii. 68, he inserts B. ii. 79—82, 84, 87, 93—95, 99, 100; in place

---

[1] This word is almost illegible, and I only guess at it. The MS. seems to have 3 down-strokes (= ui), with a fourth down-stroke (= contraction for ir?) above the central one.

of A. ii. 93, he gives us B. ii. 124 ; in place of A. iv. 100—108, he gives us B. iv. 113—125 ; after A. iv. 145, he inserts B. iv. 165—170 ; after A. v. 33, he inserts B. v. 36—41 ; after A. v. 39, we get B. v. 49—56 ; after A. v. 42, we get B. v. 60 ; after A. v. 69, we get B. v. 84—93 ; and so on. What is still more extraordinary, is the occasional introduction of lines of the C-type ; thus, after A. ii. 20, we find the insertion of two lines answering to C. iii. 28, 29 ; and after A. ii. 143, we find C. iii. 185—188. These insertions are the more remarkable because they do not occur in MS. T, to which the MS. here described bears a tolerably close *general* resemblance. The scribe has made a singular mistake at the beginning of Passus VII, which commences thus :—

Cesseþ now q*uod* þe kyng · I suffre ȝow no lengere.

This is the first line of Passus IV, wrongly repeated, as if he was going to rewrite a portion of his task. But he at once discovered the error, and proceeds with A. vii. 1 at once, as if nothing had happened. The most noteworthy variation occurs at A. xi. 163, where the scribe makes Passus XI come to an end, and inserts a new rubric ; thus :—

Tercius passus de dowel.

I went wightly my way · wiþ-oute more lettyng ; &c.

In some instances the scribe has inferior readings which impair the alliteration ; in others, he supports many of the emendations which I have already made in the text. It would be tedious to give further details about the various readings ; I will therefore merely cite a few specimens. In A. prol. 34, this MS. has *gylously* (for *giltles*) ; in A. i. 10, the latter half of the line is—*so faire was here lyre*[1] *;* in A. v. 14, the latter half of the line is—*þat so loude blew*[2] *;* in A. v. 67, the former half of the line is—*Al forbolne*[3] *for angre ;* A. v. 88 runs thus—*after þat I crie as cof*[4] · *þat god gyf hem sorwe ;* A. v. 166 ends with—*and kitte þe kempstere*[5] *;* A. v. 242 begins with—*Robyn*[6] *þe robbour.* A. vi. begins with—

ȝit were þere fewe men · þe way þeder couþe,
But blostred forþ as bestes · þrogh baches[7] and hilles.

At the end of Passus VIII there is a rubric of some importance, viz. *Sequitur prologus de dowel, dobett, et dobest.* This shows that Passus

---

[1] *lyre* = *lere*, hue, mien.
[2] This loses the mark of the date of the poem.
[3] *forbolne* = *forbollen*, greatly swollen ; from Icel. *bolginn*, swollen, with the intensive prefix *for-* ; a forcible and rare word.
[4] Again, A. vii. 104 strangely ends with—carped of cof worde. *Cof* (A.S. *cáf*) = keen, quick ; *as cof*, very quickly ; *cof* occurs nowhere else in Piers Plowman.
[5] *kempstere* = *kembstere*, a woman who combs wool ; see Prompt. Parv. ; nowhere else in our poem.
[6] Seems like an allusion to Robin Hood ; so again in A. vii. 66.
[7] For *þrogh* read *ouer ;* but *baches* is *the right reading.* See C. viii. 159.

IX (A) is really a new Prologue, and accounts for the counting of Passus X as *Passus primus de dowel.*

Of the latter part of the MS. it may suffice to say that many of its readings agree with those of S and G, sometimes with those of T, M, or F; it almost invariably differs from P and E, wherever these differ from the rest. A few lines are occasionally omitted in this portion also, viz. C. xiii. 3, 94, 105—107, 206; xiv. 45, 82, 242; xv. 18, 19, 63, 78, 122, 145; xvi. (part of) 111 and 112, 126, 210, 259, 263, 280, 281, 285, 288, 289, 303; xvii. 129, 264, 267; xviii. 116, 164, 178—180, 283, 290; xix. 159; xx. 69; xxi. 100, 255; &c. Some of these lines are omitted in other MSS., as has been already noted. The most important omission is on the back of leaf 35, where there is a gap of 66 lines (C. xiv. 110—175 inclusive) just before the fifth line from the bottom of the page. This affords positive proof that the latter part of this MS. was copied from an older one which had lost a leaf here, each page of which contained 33 lines (a common number). I note a few curious readings.

We find *Vpholsters,* C. xiii. 218; *and chynchen*[1] *but þei geten,* xiii. 227 (latter half); *I se wymmen misdo in werk · and in speche bothe,*[2] xiv. 190; *or þe licour in his coppe,* xv. 185 (latter half); *bodyngs*[3] (for *poddynges*), xvi. 66; *twynkeled*[4] (for *preynte*), xvi. 121; *Ne citalon*[5] *ne gitaron*[6] *· ne synge wiþ þe crowþe,*[7] xvi. 208; *Odibile bonum* (instead of *Distinctio paupertatis*), xvii. 121; *and here tail-end*[8] *als,* xvii. 258 (latter half); *shoris*[9] (for *shoriers*), xix. 20, 25; *sondrylopes*[10] (for *surlepes*), xix. 193; *smother,*[11] *smoþer* (for *smorþre*), xx. 305, 323; *antrous,*[12] xxi. 14; *teyned*[13] (for *tenden*), xxi. 250; *patred*[14] (for *parled*), xxi. 281; *astaroth*[15] (for *astrot*), xxi. 289; *deceyuedest*[16] (for *troiledest*), xxi. 321; *ytrolled* (for *troiled*),[17] xxi. 334; &c.

---

[1] *chynchen,* are niggardly; see Prompt. Parv. Not the right reading, but a curious word, occurring nowhere else in our poem.
[2] A very remarkable and unfair variation.
[3] I. e. puddings; F. *bouding.*
[4] I. e. winked; see Prompt. Parv.
[5] Play on the cittern; a rare verb, occurring nowhere else in our poem.
[6] Play on the gittern (the same instrument); a rare verb.
[7] Fiddle; a Welsh word; nowhere else in our poem.
[8] I. e. marking on a tally, reckoning; see the Glossary.
[9] Mod. E. *shores,* i. e. props.
[10] For *sundrilepes,* with the same force as *surlepes = serlepes;* a rare form.
[11] This gives the etymology of *smother,* which stands for *smorther.*
[12] Showing that *auntrous* is the right reading.
[13] A strange form.
[14] See Pierce the Ploughman's Crede, l. 4.
[15] Hence *astrot* really means *Ashtaroth.*
[16] A gloss upon *troiledest.*
[17] Cf. B. xviii. 296.

The following lines are curious.

    And þan frayned I at a byrde · as he sat in his nest,[1]
    To knowe dowel, quod þat byrde · and who it is, he saide
        (xiv. 220, 221).

After C. xv. 194, the following five lines are inserted (as in S) :—

    Iob was a panym · & plesed atte best,
    And Aristotle also · sewed þe same sect,
    And ladde ful holy lyf · aftre þe lawe of kynde ;
    Wherfor it semeth soþly · sondre sotels to shewe
    That he was saued so was Iob · I can not say þe soþe.

These lines can hardly be genuine; they seem to be due to imperfect reminiscence of C. xiv. 15, xii. 216—220.

XLV. A MS. in the possession of Sir Henry Ingilby, of Ripley Castle, Yorkshire. I am much indebted to Sir Henry Ingilby for kindly allowing me to inspect this MS. carefully, thus enabling me to give the extract printed above, and the very remarkable passage which I give in full below.

The date of the MS. can hardly be earlier than the middle of the fifteenth century, and there can be little doubt (I am informed) that it once belonged to a collection of MSS. in Fountains Abbey. It contains other pieces besides Piers Plowman.

    1. Þer woned a berne in babeloyne in þat burgh riche : *ends*— Of þe prophete. 4½ pages. This is the piece commonly called the 'Pistyl of Sweet Susan ; ' see the Select Remains of Scottish Poetry, ed. D. Laing, 1822.

    2. In ilke synful man or woman þat is bounden in dedly synne.[2]

    3. A treatise on the Active and Contemplative Life. (Probably by Hampole, as printed in English Prose Treatises of Richard Rolle de Hampole, ed. G. G. Perry, E. E. T. S., 1866.) The pieces 2 and 3 occupy about 21 pages.

    4. Piers Plowman ; *begins*—In a summer sesyn · whanne softe was þe sunne. This copy, which appears to be imperfect in the middle, clearly belongs to the A-text; and, as far as I can judge without a very close examination, belongs to sub-class *b*, possessing several points of similarity with MS. U and with MS. Rawl. Poet. 137. It contains one passage of much value, viz. a large portion of Passus XII, which I give at length below, on account of the great rarity of copies of this Passus. Hitherto, I have only found *one* complete copy, viz. that in MS. Rawl. Poet. 137, already printed (A-text, pp. 137*—141*). MS. U contains the first 19 lines, already collated. The Ingilby MS. contains 87 lines, answering to the first 83 lines of the Rawlinson MS. ; it omits one of these (l. 55), but, on the other hand, has five new lines, which are unique, not being extant in any other copy. At the first glance,

---

[1] *nest* is due to misunderstanding *nuste*. i. e. knew not. Hence the scribe had to alter both lines, without obtaining much sense after all.

[2] Another copy in MS. W ; see B-text, Pref. p. xiii.

I had hopes of recovering a new copy of the whole of this rare twelfth Passus, and was particularly anxious to see the exact point at which the Passus was completed; it was somewhat disappointing to find that just the last few lines, the most important, are wanting. It is clear that the scribe had an imperfect copy before him. He did his best, writing the last line upon a new page; but he evidently had no more to copy from, and had to leave the rest of the page blank. We want just 17 lines more, but they are not to be had from this source. It is, however, a considerable gain that he has given us so much; for we are now assured that this " Passus Tercius de Dowel " was the Passus with which the A-text originally concluded. As every scrap of information about this Passus is important from its rarity, I here give it as it stands in this MS.

Passus tercius de dowel.

"Crist wote," qu*o*d clergy · " know it ʒif the like,
I haue don my deuer · the dowele to teche;
An[d] ho-so couetyth bene bet*er* · than the boke tellyth,
He passyth the apostillis lyue · & peryth to angel*is*.   4
But I se now, I seye · as me soth thinkyth,
The were leue for to lerne · but loth for to stodye;
Thou woldyst cony*n* that I can · & carpyn it aft*er*,
Presumptuusly, p*ar* auenture · aposyn so manye,   8
That myht t*ur*n me to tene · & theologye bothin.
ʒif I wist witterly · thou wyldyst don th*er*-after,
Al that t' ou axist · asoylyn I wolde."
Scornfull ʃhe scripture · tho schet vp her browes,   12
And on clergye criyd · on cristye holy halue,
That he it schewe me nout schold · but I schriuen were
Of the kynde cardenal · & cristenyd in a founte;
And seyd [it] so lowyd · that schame me thowte,   16
" That it wer scathe & sclaunder · to al holy cherche,
Sethin teologye, that true is · to tellyn it defendyth;
Dauid, goddys derlyng · defendith it also,
  Vidi preuaricantes, et tabescebam:
' I sayhe synful,' he seyde · therfor I seyde no-thing,   20
Til tho wrecches ben in wille · her synne to lete;
And powle p*r*eched it oftyn · p*r*estys it redyn,
  Audiui archana verba, que non licet homini loqui:
' I am not hardy,' qu*o*d he · of that I herd wi*th* erys
Tellyn it wi*th* tong · to synful schrewys.   24
And god gr*a*untyd neu*er* · the gospel it witnessith
In the passyou*n*, how pylat · aposyd god almyht,
And axed i*e*su on hye · th*er* herdyn it an hunderith,
' *Quid est veritas*,' quod he · ' veriliche tel vs?'   28

4. *Peryth*, is a peer (to); a good reading.
9. *Turn*; written 't*u*run.'
12. *Schet*; read *set*.
13. MS. name halue, *with* name ex-P. PLOWMAN, NO. 17.

   *pu*ɴ*oted; but* name *is right*.
14. The reading *I schriuen* is perhaps the right one.
16. We must supply *it*.
22. *P*r*eched* seems the better reading.

MANUSCRIPTS OF PIERS PLOWMAN.

God ȝaf him none answere · but gan his tung holde.
Ri[h]t so I rede," quod sche · " rede thou no ferthere
Of that he ȝernyth to wyte ׃ wysse him no beter;
For he can nouth be cause · to lernyn to dowele,   32
But als ho seyth, swyche I am · qwan he with men Iangelyth."
And qwan scripture the scolde had this scole schewyd,
Clergy in-to caban · crepe anone after,
And drowe the dore to him · & bad me go dowele,   36
Or wykly, ȝif I wolde · qwethir that me lykyd !
Than held I vp myn hondes · to scripture the wyse,
To bene her man, ȝif I most · for euere-more after,
With that sche wolde me wissyn · qwere the toune were   40
That kynd wytte the confessoure · her kynnysman was Inne
That lady than lowhe on me · & lawht me in her armys,
And seyd, " my cosyn kynd wit · knowyn is ful wyde
And is lyggyng with lyfe · that lorde is of erthe.   44
And ȝif thou desyre · with him for to dwelle,
I schal the wyssyn wynlyche · qwere that he dwellyth."
And than I knelyd on my knes · & kyssyd here fete sone,
A thowsyng tymes I thankyd hire · with throbbyng hert.   48
Sche callyd a clergyn than that hi[h]te
Omnia-probate · a pore thing with-alle ;
" Thou schalt wendyn with wille " · quod sche, " qwyl him lykyth,
Tyl ȝe come to the bo[ro]whe · quod-bonum-est-tenete ;   52
Kenne him to my cosynys howce · that kynde wit hi[h]te ;
Sey I sent him this segge · & that he schew him dowele."

. . . .

I went forth in my wey · with omnia-probate;   56
Er I kam to the contreyys · quod-bonum-est-tenete,
Many ferlyys me befel · in a fewe ȝeris.
The fyrst ferly I fonde · an-hunger[d] it me made,
And I than [ȝede] thorow ȝowthe · aȝeyn prime dayes.   60
I stode stil in a stody · & stared a-boute ;
" Al heyle," quod on thoo · I seyd, " welcom ! and with hom be
  ȝowe ? "
" I am dwellyng with deth · & hunger I hy[h]te ;
To lyf & his lordschep · longyth my weye,   64
To kyllyn him, ȝif I can ; · thei kynde wit helpe,
I schalle fellyn that freyke · in a fewe dayes."
" I wold folwyn the fayne," quod I · " but fayntys me hentith,

32. For can read cam, i. e. came.
33. Perhaps als ho is the better reading.
34. For scole read skile (perhaps written soele) : this is certainly the correct reading. It means 'this reason.'
41. The insertion of That makes the sense clear.
46. The insertion of wynlyche renders the line complete.
48. For thowsyng read thowsand.

49. This line is still faulty. MS. hite (and in l. 53).
52. MS. bowhe ; for borowhe.
55. This line is missing.
59. MS. an hunger.
60. MS. omits ȝede.
62. For hom read whom.
63. MS. hyte ; cf. ll. 49, 53.
65. A new line. thei = though, although.
67. The insertion of quod I makes the sense clear.

MANUSCRIPTS OF PIERS PLOWMAN. 31

Me folwyth such a fayntyse · I may not forth walke." 68
"Go we forth," quod the gome · "I haue a gret boyste
Of battys & brokyn bred · thi bely to fille,
A bagge-ful, of a beggar · I bowht it at onys."
Than maungyd I with him · vp to the fulle ; 72
For myssyng of mete · none mesur I cowthe,
But ete as hunger me hete · til my belly swellyd.
Ther bad me hunger 'haue gode day' · but I helde me stille ;
For gronyng of my guttys · I durst gon no ferther. 76
With that kam a knaue · with a confessours face,
Lene & rewlyche · with leggys ful smale ;
I haylsyd hym hendely · & axid him after,
Of qwennys that he were · & qwedyr that he wolde. 80
"With deth I dwelle," quod he · "dayys & nyhetys ;
My name is feuer ; on the ferthe day · I am athirst euere.
I am mensenger of deth · men haue I twayne.
That on is callyd cotidian · a currur of oure howce ; 84
Tertyen that othyr · true drinkers bothen ;
We haue letterys of his lyf · he schal his lyf tyne,
Fro deth, that is oure duke · swyche dedys we bryng.
Myht I se," quod he, "god wote · ȝoure gatys wold I holdyn. 88
[*The rest is wanting.*]

70. *Battys*, fragments, pieces ; a good word.
72. This line is still unsatisfactory.
74—76. Three new lines.
78. A new line.

79. A much better line than that in the other copy.
82. For *athirst* read *afurst*.
86. *tyne ;* the right reading, as I expected.
88. For *se* read *so ;* for *he* read *I*.

KEY TO THE ABOVE LIST OF MSS.

1. For the numbers of the MSS., see p. 4.
2. For the meanings of the letters denoting certain MSS., see p. 6.
3. In the Parallel Extracts, pp. 6—24, the MSS. are arranged in the following order, according to their actual value.

A-text. Sub-class *a*. I. II. Sub-class *b*. XI. XII. IV. XLV. Sub-class *c*. III. V. XLIV. VI. VII. VIII. Sub-class *d*. IX. X.
B-text. *a*. XIII. XVII. XIV. *b*. XVI. XXI. XXII. XXIII. XXIV. XXV. *c*. XVIII. XIX. *d*. XV.* XXVII. XV. *a*, *b*, *c*, or *d*. XX. *e*. XXVI. *f*. XXVIII.
C-text. *a*. XXIX. XXX. XXXI. XXXV. XXXVI. XLI. XLII. *b*. XXXII. XXXIX. XXXVIII. (III. V. XLIV. X ; *also* XXIII—XXV). *a*. or *b*. XL. *c*. XXXVII. *d*. XXXIII. *e*. XXXIV. XLIII.

LIST OF FIRST LINES OF THE PASSUS OF PIERS PLOWMAN.

Since *Passus* of the Poem are often not numbered in the MSS., or else, perhaps, so numbered as not to adhere to the same system throughout, the following list of first lines is added, as likely to be of great use to the reader of a MS. in finding his place. It will be noticed that those of the Vernon type (A-text) divide *Passus* V. of the Crowley type (B-text) into *two Passus;* whilst *Passus* VI. of the Whitaker type (C-text) begins with 108 lines which are peculiar to MSS. of that type.

A. *Passus of the Vernon MS.*

Prol. In A somer sesun · whon softe was þe sonne.
I. What þis Mountein be-Meneþ · and þis derke Dale.
II. Yit kneled I on my knees · and cried hire of grace.
III. Now is Meede þe Mayden I-nomen · *and* no mo of hem alle.
IV. Seseþ seide þe kyng · I suffre ȝou no more.
V. Þe kyng and his knihtes · to þe Churche wenten.
VI. Bote þer were fewe men so wys · þat coupe þe wei þider.[1]
VII. Þis weore a wikked wei · bote hose hedde a gyde.
VIII. Treuþe herde telle her-of · And to Pers sende.
Incipit hic Dowel. Dobet. and Dobest.
(IX). *Prol.* Þus I-Robed in Russet · Romed I a-boute.
(X). I. (*Do-wel*) Sire Do-wel dwelleþ quod wit · not a day hennes.
(XI). II. (*Do-wel*) Þenne hedde wit A wyf · was hoten dam Studie.
(XII). III. (*Do-wel*) Crist wot quod clergie · knowe hit ȝif þe lyke.[2]

---

[1] MS. H alone prefixes two lines to the line here quoted, viz.
    Now riden þis folk · & walken on fote
    To seche þat seint · in selcouþe londis.
[2] Not in the Vernon MS.; found in MS. Rawl. Poet. 137. Some MSS., instead of this Passus, actually have Pass. XIII—XXIII of the C-text. See vol. i. p. xviii., and p. 29 above.

B. Passus of the Crowley Type of MSS. (MS. Laud 581.)

Prol. In a somer seson · whan soft was the sonne.
I. What this montaigne bymeneth · and þe merke dale.
II. Yet I courbed on my knees · and cryed hir of grace.
III. Now is Mede the Mayde · and namo of hem alle.
IV. Cesseth, seith the kynge · I suffre ȝow no lengere.
V. The kyng and his knightes · to the kirke wente.
VI. This were a wikked way · but who-so hadde a gyde.
VII. Treuthe herde telle her-of · and to peres he sent.

ends—*Explicit visio willelmi de petro plowman : et sequitur vita de dowell, dobett et do-beste secundum wytt et reson ;* MS. C2.

VIII. (or *Prologus* to *Do-wel*) Thus y-robed in russet · I romed aboute.
IX. (I. *Do-wel*) Sire Do-wel dwelleth, quod witte · nouȝt a day hennes.
X. (II. *Do-wel*) Thanne hadde witte a wyf · was hote dame studye.
XI. (III. *Do-wel*) Thanne scripture scorned me · and a skile tolde.
XII. (IV. *Do-wel*) I am ymaginatyf, quod he · Idel was I neuere.
XIII. (V. *Do-wel*) And I awaked þere-with · witles nerehande.
XIV. (VI. *Do-wel*) I haue but one [hool] hatere quod haukyn · I am þe lasse to blame.

ends—*Finit dowel, et incipit dobet.*

XV. (*Prologus* to *Do-bet*) Ac after my wakyng · it was wonder longe.
XVI. (I. *Do-bet*) Now faire falle ȝow quod I þo · for ȝowre faire shewynge.
XVII. (II. *Do-bet*) I am spes quod he a spye · and spire after a knyȝte.
XVIII. (III. *Do-bet*) Wolleward and weteshoed · went I forth after.

ends—*Explicit do-bet, et incipit do-best.*

XIX. (*Prologus* to *Do-best*) Thus I awaked & wrote · what I had dremed.
XX. (I. *Do-best*) Thanne as I went by þe way · whan I was þus awaked.

ends—*Explicit hic dialogus petri plowman.*

C. Passus of the MS. printed by Whitaker.

(*Hic Incipit Visio Willelmi de Petro Plouhman.*)

I. In a somere seyson · whan softe was þe sonne.
II. What þe montayne by-meneþ · and þe merke dale.
III. And þanne ich knelede on my knees · and cryede to hure of grace.[1]
IV. Now is mede the mayde · and no mo of hem alle.

[1] Some MSS. follow the C-text as far as iii. 13, after which they follow the B-text beginning with B. ii. 121. See vol. ii. p. 392.

LIST OF FIRST LINES OF THE PASSUS.

V. Cesseþ, saide þe kyng · ich soffre ȝow no lenger.
VI. Thus ich a-waked wot god · wanne ich wonede on corne-hulle.
VII. With þat ran repentaunce · and reherced hus teme.
VIII. Tho cam sleuthe al by-slobered · wit to slymed eyen.
IX. Tho sayde perken plouhman · by seynt peter of rome.
X. Treuthe herde telle here-of · and to peers sente.
  ends—*Hic explicit Visio Willī de Petro Plouhman.*
  Incipit visio ejusdem Willī de Dowel.
(XI). I. Thus robed in russett · ich romede a-boute.
(XII). II. Thenne hadde wit a wif · was hote dame studie.
(XIII). III. Alas eye quath elde · and holynesse boþe.
(XIV). IV. Ac wel worth pouerte · for he may walke vnrobbede.
(XV). V. Ich am ymaginatif quaþ he · ydel was ich neuere.
(XVI). VI. And ich awakede þer-with · wittlees ner hande.
(XVII). VII. Alas that riche[sse] shal reue · and robbe mannes soule.
  ends—*Hic explicit Passus Septimus et Ultimus de Dowel.*
  Incipit Passus Primus de Dobet.
(XVIII). I. Ther is no suche ich seide · þat som tyme ne borweth.
(XIX). II. Leue *liberum arbitrium* quaþ ich · ich leyue as ich hope.
(XX). III. Ich am spes quaþ he · and spirr after a knyght.
(XXI). IV. Wo-werie and wetschode · wente ich forth after.
  ends—*Hic explicit Passus Quartus et Ultimus de Dobet.*
  Hic incipit Passus Primus de Dobest.
(XXII). I. Thus ich awakede and wrot · what ich hadde dremed.
(XXIII). II. And as ich wente by þe waye · when ich was þus awakede.
  ends—*Hic explicit Passus Secundus de Dobest. Explicit Peeres Plouheman.*

The manufacturer's authorised representative in the EU for product safety is Oxford University Press España S.A. of El Parque Empresarial San Fernando de Henares, Avenida de Castilla, 2 - 28830 Madrid (www.oup.es/en or product.safety@oup.com). OUP España S.A. also acts as importer into Spain of products made by the manufacturer.
Printed and bound by CPI Group (UK) Ltd, Croydon, CR0 4YY

20/03/2026

02075340-0002